INTERNATIONAL CENTRE FOR MECHANICAL SCIENCES

COURSES AND LECTURES - No. 88

FABRIZIO LUCCIO
UNIVERSITY OF PISA

AN INTRODUCTION TO THE THEORY OF AUTOMATA

COURSE HELD AT THE DEPARTMENT
FOR AUTOMATION AND INFORMATION
JULY 1971

UDINE 1971

SPRINGER-VERLAG WIEN GMBH

ISBN 978-3-211-81082-8   ISBN 978-3-7091-2816-9 (eBook)
DOI 10.1007/978-3-7091-2816-9

Copyright 1971 by Springer-Verlag Wien
Originally published by Springer Vienna in 1971

PREFACE

In the short extension of five lectures, we try to summarize some of the basic notions of Automata Theory.

Our concern throughout these notes has been the use of an understandable form of presentation, without loss of rigor. Frequent examples are discussed, and some simple exercises have been inserted in the text, mainly as tests for comprehension.

Since the field of automata has grown up to a considerable size, some topics have been purposedly ignored: among them, Turing machines constitute the most spectacular omission. In fact, such machines are illustrated in a companion set of lectures, while emphasis is given here to the System Theory approach to automata, along the lines indicated by Kalman, Falb and Arbib in [5].

It must be noted, however, that Automata Theory has been deeply influenced by parallel studies on sequential networks, since the pioneering work of Huffman and Moore on the theoretical bases of data processors. Several aspects of our models will be seen in this light, according to the classical textbook by Ginsburg [3]. Then, to demonstrate the flexibility of automata, a number of examples will be taken from different fields of application.

At the end of these lectures, the student will just gain a glance on the vast world of automata. A rich literature – in particular, the superb last effort of Arbib [1] – is then at his disposal, to help him entering the field.

I wish to conclude warmly thanking CISM for its invitation to deliver these lectures, in a unique atmosphere of international cooperation on high scientific standing.

F. L.

Udine, July 1971

1. Introduction: Automata and Systems.

In the process of evolution that the science continuously follows, two facts are relevant to the study that we are going to undertake: namely

i. the icreasing power of an abstract mathematical model, the <u>automaton</u>, as to cover a variety of different entities;

and, on a higher level,

ii. the massive growth of System Theory as a unifying discipline, to encompass a number of topics falling in the classical range of "Mathematics for Engineers".

Since i. and ii. are recent facts, the confluence of Automata Theory into System Theory is a very recent but perfectly legitimate result.

In the consequent perspective, the automaton is seen as a system of special nature, evolving in discrete times through discrete points of the state space. Such a vantage position has been strongly assumed by Kalman, Falb and Arbib [5], and will be adopted here for a general observation of the automaton behavior. As a result, such notions as <u>controllability</u> and <u>observability</u> on one side, <u>equivalence</u> and <u>minimization</u> on the other, will be studied in a common framework, though originally pertaining to the different fields of System and Automata Theory. The unifying tool will be the (simulated) experimentation on the model.

Since most of the recent literature on automata is nearly incomprehensible by the non specialist, a continuous effort will be made throughout these notes to render the matter as understandable as possible. However, clearity will be sought for by methodical use of working examples, no concession being made to lowering the mathematical rigor of the discussion.

In addition, some significant materialization of the abstract automaton will be indicated.

2. The notion of state.

Before being seen in the general form of a system, the automaton has moved many steps in its birth field of electrical engineering. It would be naive - besides ungrateful - to forget such an origin, and in particular the tight relation between automata and sequential networks, since many aspects of the first have been studied to support the development of the second. In fact, Automata Theory has reached its present stage mainly because of the impact of computers on today's society: as well as, for example, other branches of Mathematics have flourished in connection with the needs of Nuclear Physics.

If used to model a digital network, the automaton is seen as a "black box", where the mere relation between input and output signals is relevant to the external world. However,

Formal definition of system

if the automaton is studied as a dynamic system, primary emphasis is to be given to the notions of <u>state</u>, evolution through states, controllability of a state.

That is, a tendency arises to assign a phisical reality to a concept – the state – that was customarily regarded as a <u>descriptive mean</u> of the machine behavior.

In fact, the description of the automaton as a translator of input into output sequences, must take into account that any single output signal is a function of the input history, that is of all the input signals up to that moment. This is easily achieved by postulating the existence of states for the automaton, such that any state bears by hypothesis a complete memory of the past history. Suitable laws are derived for determining the next state assumed by the machine, when a new input signal is applied, as well as the output signal generated in such event. Since, in any moment, the effect of previous input signals is taken into account by the present state, both the output and the next state will be simply evaluated as functions of the preset input and state.

All the above notions will now be put in a neat mathematical form. According to a standard notation, a <u>system</u> S to work in continuous time is defined as a formal quintuple:

$$S = (\Omega, Y, Q, \lambda, \delta) \tag{1}$$

where:

Ω is the set of input segments: $\omega \in \Omega$ is an admissible input signal applied for a finite interval of time $t_o - t$;

Y is the set of outputs;

Q is the set of states;

λ is a mapping of $Q \times \Omega$ into Q (*) indicated by:
by: $\lambda : Q \times \Omega \to Q$.

is a mapping of $Q \times \Omega$ onto Q (*) indicated by:
by: $\delta : Q \times \Omega \to Y$.

The interpretation of (1) is the one of a system which, in state $q \in Q$ at time t_o , will react to the input segment ω applied during the interval $t_o - t$, by assuming the state $\lambda(q,\omega) \in Q$ and generating the output $\delta(q,\omega) \in Y$ at the time t.

Although some of the properties which will be derived are valid in the general case of a system of the above type, we will immediately restrict our field of study to the class of automata, by imposing some restrictions over the quintuple (1); namely:

i. the functioning of the system is studied in <u>discrete time</u>; that is, in consecutive moments, identifiable as $t = 0, 1 \ldots$ on a suitable discrete scale;

ii. Ω is <u>finite</u>;

(*) The notation $A \times B$ denotes the cartesian product of sets A and B, that is the set of all the pairs a, b such that $a \in A$, $b \in B$.

iii. Y is finite.

While constraint iii. does not bear any message of particular importance, some basic facts about the automaton nature are substantiated by constraints i. and ii. In fact: i'. being the time discrete implies that any input segment ω is a discrete sequence of signals; and: ii'. being Ω finite implies that such sequences are finite in number, that is the set X of input signals is finite. This last implication shows that Ω becomes coincident with the set X^* of all the possible sequences of finite length, composed on the set X under concatenation of its elements. (*)

Since X^* can be directly derived from X, this last set substitutes Ω in the definition of automaton, which is derived as follows from the given definition of system.

Definition 1. An automaton A is a quintuple:

$$A = (X, Y, Q, \lambda, \delta) \qquad (2)$$

where:

X is the finite set of input signals (or inputs);
Y is the finite set of output signals (or outputs);
Q is the set of states;
$\lambda : Q \times X \to Q$;
$\delta : Q \times X \to Y$.

(*) In the semigroup theory of automata [5], X^* would be the "free semigroup on X".

2. The notion of state

The interpretation of (2) is the one of a machine which, in state $q_i \in Q$ at time t, will react to the input $x_j \in X$, by assuming at time $t + 1$ the new state $\lambda(q_i, x_j) \in Q$ and generating the output $\delta(q_i, x_j) \in Y$.

λ and δ are respectively called <u>next state function</u> and <u>output function</u>. They specify the next state and output at any step of an input sequence $x_j^* \in X^*$; then, extending their definition as:

(3)
$$\lambda : Q \times X^* \to Q$$
$$\delta : Q \times X^* \to Y$$

is legitimate by the obvious validity of the relations:

(4)
$$\lambda(q_i, x_j^* x_k^*) = \lambda(\lambda(q_i, x_j^*), x_k^*)$$
$$\delta(q_i, x_j^* x_k^*) = \delta(\lambda(q_i, x_j^*), x_k^*)$$

where $x_j^*, x_k^* \in X^*$.

Some important considerations are now in order, on the finiteness of the problems that we are going to face.

If Q is finite, A is called a <u>finite automaton</u>. Unless differently stated, we shall deal with finite automata.

X is finite by definition. However, X^* could not be finite if the sequences x_i^* are allowed not to be finite (thus violating some previous assumptions). It is an interesting issue to discuss the relationship between the finiteness of Q and X; an important example in such respect will be given with a lin-

A traditional visualization of automata

guistic interpretation of automata.

To make the following formal steps more understandable, a graphic representation of the model can be very helpful. According to a traditional visualization, a finite automaton A is represented as a direct graph G, having a node n_i for any state $q_i \in Q$. To any branch of G connecting n_i to n_j, the pair x_r/y_s is associated, such that $\lambda(q_i, x_r) = q_j$ and $\delta(q_i, x_r) = y_s$. For example, the simple automaton:

$$A = (X, Y, Q, \lambda, \delta)$$

where:

$$X = \{x_1, x_2\}$$

$$Y = \{y_1, y_2\}$$

$$Q = \{q_1, q_2, q_3, q_4\}$$

Q × X	λ	δ
q_1, x_1	q_2	y_1
q_1, x_2	q_3	y_2
q_2, x_1	q_1	y_1
q_2, x_2	q_3	y_2
q_3, x_1	q_2	y_2
q_3, x_2	q_1	y_1
q_4, x_1	q_1	y_2
q_4, x_2	q_2	y_1

is represented in the compact form:

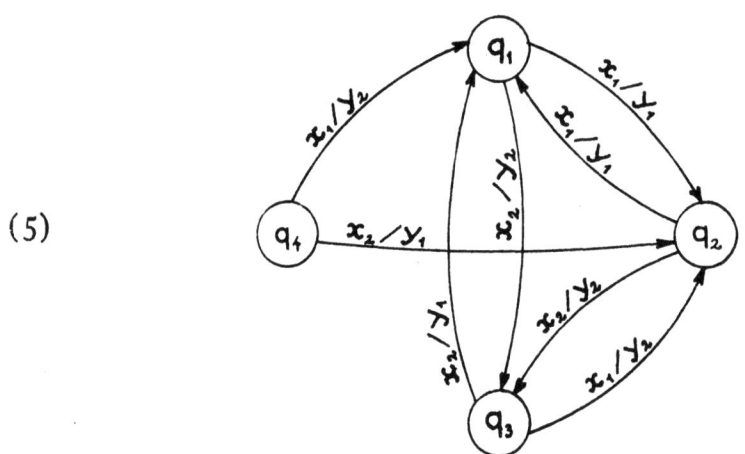

(5)

(5) is still an abstract example. Let us tentatively assert that the simplest materialization of an automaton in common use is the ball point pen P, whose terminal push button controls the alternative appearences and desappearences of the point. If seen as a black box, the pen has one input "push" representing the operation of the push button, and two outputs "in" and "out" representing the positions of the point. The word specification of the functioning is: whenever an input appears, the output changes its value. (*)

(*) In the present case, inputs and outputs are different in nature: the input lasts for given intervals of time, while the outputs last for intervals of any length, just until a new input occurs. In the theory of sequential networks, such signals would be respectively called "pulses" and "levels". (In such a theory, the ball point pen would probably be called "flip flop").

Basic definitions and terminology 13

For describing P as an automaton A, it is convenient to introduce two states q_1 and q_2 with the assumption that, whenever A is steady in q_1 (or q_2), the output is maintained at the value "in" (or "out"). Then, the ball point pen is represented as:

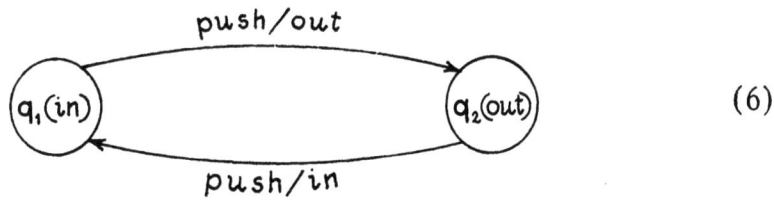

(6)

To conclude this section on the notion of state, we note that the automata considered thus far are <u>stationary</u> and <u>deterministic</u>.

The condition of being stationary is the <u>time invariance</u> of the functions λ and δ : such time invariance actually substantiates the validity of the extended definitions (3).

The conditions of being deterministic is that the next state of the automaton is exactly determined in any circumstance: that is, λ is a mapping of $Q \times X$ into Q. Such a property will be subject to a further discussion.

Finally, two definitions are in order.

<u>Definition 2.</u> A state q_j is <u>reachable</u> from another state q_i if and only if there exists a sequence $x^* \in X^*$, such that (extended definition of λ):

$$q_j = \lambda(q_i, x^*).$$

Definition 3. An automaton A is <u>strongly connected</u> if every state of A is reachable from every other state.

For example, state q_3 of automaton (5) is reachable from q_4, since there exists the sequence $x_1 x_2$ such that:

$$q_3 = \lambda(q_4, x_1, x_2).$$

However, the automaton is not strongly connected, since q_4 is not reachable from any other state. It may be noted that the automaton obtained from (5) by suppressing state q_4 (and all the transitions between q_4 and any other state) is strongly connected.

3. Equivalence and minimization.

In nearly all the applications of automata theory, a crucial problem is the one of determining the "minimal" automaton which is "equivalent" to a given one. The term minimal can be simply - and traditionally - taken as being synonim of "fewest-state" (even though an extension of this concept to the combined state-input reduction has been proposed [6]). The term equivalent, instead, is to be carefully defined.

Such a definition must be ultimately based on the observation of the terminal behavior of the automata under consideration, that is on the relation of input to output sequences, thus requiring the simulation of experiments on the systems. However, the notion of state will be of great importance to neatly represent the problem, even though the experiments must prescind any knowledge of state.

Let

$$P = (X_p, Y_p, Q_p, \lambda_p, \delta_p)$$
$$S = (X_s, Y_s, Q_s, \lambda_s, \delta_s)$$
(7)

be automata, where small p and small s will be reserved to indicate the states of P and S respectively, and let

$$X_p = X_s \text{ (that implies } X_p^* = X_s^*).$$

<u>Definition 4.</u> A state p of P is <u>equivalent</u> to a state s of S if, for every sequence x^*, $\delta_p(p, x^*) = \delta_s(s, x^*)$.

In symbols, the equivalence is indicated as $p \equiv s$. If P is coincident with S, the equivalence is defined between states of a single automaton.

For example, $q_1 \equiv q_2$ in the automaton (5). In fact, any input sequence x^* can be expressed as:

$$x^* = x_1^* x_2^* x_3^*$$

where

$$x_1^* = x_1 x_1 x_1 \ldots, \quad x_2^* = x_2, \quad x_3^* = \text{any string};$$

and any of x_1^*, x_2^*, x_3^* may be void. The output sequence y^*, generated in response to x^*, is for both q_1 and q_2 :

$$y^* = y_1 y_1 y_1 \ldots y_2 \bar{y}^*$$

3. Equivalence and minimization

That is, at any step, $\delta(q_1, \bar{x}^*) = \delta(q_2, \bar{x}^*)$, where $\bar{x}^*$ is any subsequence of x^*.

Exercise. Construct two simple automata P, S such that:

$X_P = X_S$; $Q_P = \{p_1, p_2\}$; $Q_S = \{s_1, s_2\}$; $p_1 \equiv s_1$, and no other equivalence between states holds.

It can be easily shown (Def. 4) that the following properties are valid for the equivalence:

$p \equiv p$ for every state p (reflexivity);

if $p \equiv s$, then $s \equiv p$ (symmetry);

if $p \equiv s$ and $s \equiv r$, then $p \equiv r$ (transitivity).

Then, for a single automaton A, $\equiv$ is an <u>algebraic equivalence</u> relation on the set Q of states. That is, if q is a typical element of Q, $\{q\} = \{q_i \mid q_i \equiv q\}$ is the <u>equivalence class</u> of q generated by $\equiv$; the family of such equivalence classes is a <u>partition</u> of Q. (*)

(*) Remember that a partition of a set S is a collection $S_1, S_2, \ldots, S_s$ of pairwise disjoint subsets of S whose union is S that is:

$S_i \cap S_j$ is void, for any $i \neq j$;
$\bigcup_i S_i = S$ for $i = 1, 2, \ldots, s$.

Each subset S_i is called a <u>block</u> of the partition.

For example, the automaton:

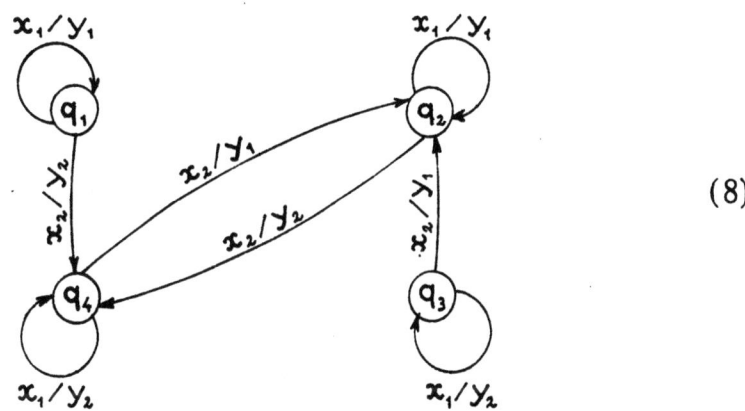

(8)

exhibits the obvious equivalences: $q_1 \equiv q_2$, $q_3 \equiv q_4$. Then, $\{q_1, q_2\}$ and $\{q_3, q_4\}$ are the equivalence classes generated by $\equiv$; $\{q_1, q_2\}$, $\{q_3, q_4\}$ is the corresponding partition of the set of states.

An interesting property of $\equiv$ is that, if two states p, s are equivalent, so are the ones into which the automata are led by the application of the same input sequence, starting from p and s. More formally, for two automata P and S defined as in (7) (possibly, P coincident with S), the proposition holds:

Proposition 1. Let p be a state of P, s be a state of S, $p \equiv s$.
Then, $\lambda_P(p, x^*) \equiv \lambda_S(s, x^*)$, for any input sequence x^*.
Exercise. Derive a proof for Proposition 1.

For the automata (5) and (8), only trivial applications of Proposition 1 are possible.

3. Equivalence and minimization

We are now in the position to formulate a precise definition of equivalence between automata; that is, to give the conditions under which different automata have identical terminal behavior.

Definition 5. Two automata P and S are <u>equivalent</u>, if and only if for each state $p \in Q_p$ there is a state $s \in Q_s$ such that $p \equiv s$ and vice versa.

Since no confusion arises, the same symbol used in connection with the states will be adopted to indicate the equivalence of automata, namely $P \equiv S$. Clearly, the equivalence between automata also exhibits the properties of reflexivity, symmetry and transitivity, thus being an algebraic equivalence relation, and partitioning any set of automata into equivalence classes.

Note that Definition 5 does not require that for each p there is exactly one s, $p \equiv s$, or vice versa. That is, $\#(Q_p)$ and $\#(Q_s)$ need not be equal. (*)

For example the automaton

(9)

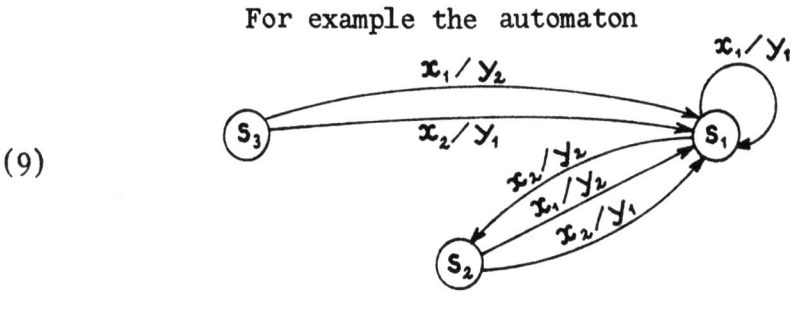

(*) For a set A, $\#(A)$ denotes the number of elements (or ./.

is equivalent to the automaton (5), since the equivalences between states hold:

$$q_1 \equiv s_1 \; ; \quad q_2 \equiv s_1 \; ; \quad q_3 \equiv s_2 \; ; \quad q_4 \equiv s_3 \; .$$

The reader may easily verify the above relations by himself.

The equivalence between two automata (Def. 5) is then based on the equivalence of their states, which is in turn individuated (Def. 4) by studying the response of the automata to "any sequence $\bar{x}^*$". Even if an upper bound to the length of input sequences is given (hence, X^* is finite), the number of such sequences is generally so large, to put out of any reasonable consideration an exhaustive experimentation. Furthermore, if X^* is not finite, the nature itself of the above definitions is not finitary.

However, some fundamental results of automata theory allow to constrict the problem in finite terms. Let us report here only the ones related to the equivalence between states of a single automaton, upon which the process of minimization will be based.

Let A be an automaton, $n = \#(Q)$ be the number of its states, $q_i, q_j \in Q$.

Theorem 1. $q_i \equiv q_j$ if and only if $\delta(q_i, \bar{x}^*) = \delta(q_j, \bar{x}^*)$ for every input sequence $\bar{x}^*$ of length $\leq n - 1$.

---

cardinality) of A.

A proof of this theorem can be found in Ginsburg [3], Ch. 1. A classical example shows that $n-1$ actually is the best bound, that is sequences of length $n-1$ may be necessary in the general case. Namely, consider the automaton:

(10)

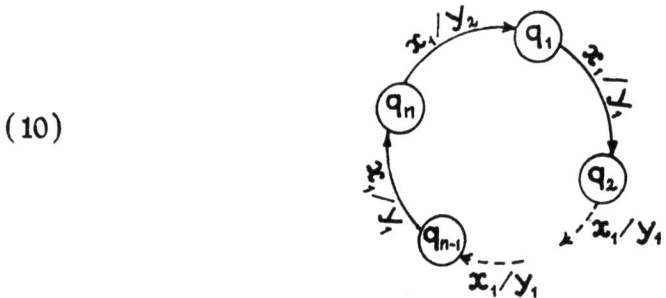

whose input sequences are merely strings of x_1's. The states q_1 and q_2 are not equivalent, since they yield different outputs in response to an input sequence $x^*_{(n-1)}$ of length $n-1$:

$$\delta(q_1, x^*_{(n-1)}) = y_1 \; ; \qquad \delta(q_2, x^*_{(n-1)}) = y_2 \; ;$$

while any sequence of smaller length would yield the same output y_1.

For automaton (5), the relation $q_1 = q_2$ has been derived by ad hoc reasoning, as an example of direct application of definition 4. However to construct a reasoning of such a kind would be impossible in the general case. In fact, by theorem 1 only input sequences of maximum length 3 can be used to determine all state equivalences.

By trying such sequences, the reader may easily verify that the relation $q_3 = q_4$ is also valid, while no other

The problem of minimality

equivalence holds between states of (5). Then, the partition of states of (5) in equivalence classes is:

$$\{q_1, q_2\} \;,\; \{q_3, q_4\} \;.$$

The results derived thus are now sufficient to treat the problem of minimality.

Definition 6. An automaton A is in <u>minimal form</u>, if it contains no two equivalent states.

Assertion 1. For any given automaton A, there exists exactly one automaton A' in minimal form, which is equivalent to A (*).

A' can be constructed by deriving all the equivalence classes for A, and associating any of such classes to a state of A'. Inputs and outputs of A' are consequently assigned.

For automaton (5), whose equivalence classes have already been determined as $\{q_1, q_2\}$ and $\{q_3, q_4\}$, the following equivalent automaton in minimal form can be constructed, where the state s_1 is associated to $\{q_1, q_2\}$, the state s_2 is associated to $\{q_3, q_4\}$:

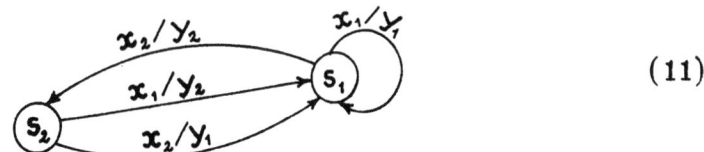

(11)

(*) A' is uniquely determined up to an isomorphism. That is, there exists other automata satisfying Assertion 1, which are obtainable from A' by mere relabeling of its states.

Application. By using the above notions, model a simple electrical network that performs the following task. A lamp L is operated by a power supply, and controlled by two switches S_1 and S_2. The lamp has two states: off-on. The sxitches have two positions: open - closed (indicated by o - c). In any condition, L changes its state by moving anyone of the switches (S_1 and S_2 cannot be moved contemporarily).

We must consider four inputs, namely oo, oc, co, cc, corresponding to the possible positions of $S_1 S_2$; and two outputs, namely off, on, corresponding to the conditions of L. In designing the network, the two state automaton (12.a) can be used:

(12.a)   (12.b)

where q_1 and q_2 respectively correspond to the "states" off and on of L. However, $q_1 \equiv q_2$, and the equivalent minimal automaton (12.b) can be constructed.

(12.b) is a pathological case, having one state only. The interpretation of this fact is that the input/output behavior actually does not depend upon history of the circuit. In fact, in any moment the output is a function of the present input only (in electrical terms, the circuit is "combinatorial").

Determining the equivalence classes of states

Then, minimizing of the model shows the real nature of a system, whose functioning description in terms of evolution through states may appear intuitively correct.

Exercise (voluntary). Design the electrical connections for the above circuit, and derive a good sense justification that no memory function is involved. (Should you have at home a lamp operated by two switches, you may dismount the network and look into it).

Assertion 1 takes different forms in the literature, and is frequently regarded as a theorem. It appeared in the early papers on sequential machines, as a basis for the so-called "state merging techniques".

All such techniques actually offer a systematic way of determining the equivalence classes of states for a given automaton. Among them, the Paull and Unger procedure is worth to be mentioned. An equivalence table is constructed, having a cell (q_i, q_j) for every couple of internal states q_i, q_j. Such a cell is used to carry the conditions for equivalence between the corresponding states; namely:

i. If $\delta(q_i, x_h) \neq \delta(q_j, x_h)$ for some input x_h, q_i and q_j are directly recognized not to be equivalent, and a corresponding mark (e.g., a cross) is entered in cell (q_i, q_j).

ii. If $\delta(q_i, x_h) = \delta(q_j, x_h)$ for all x_h, then q_i and q_j may be equivalent, and all the distinct couples of distinct next states q_r, q_s where $q_r = \lambda(q_i, x_h)$, $q_s = \lambda(q_j, x_h)$ are registered in cell (q_i, q_j). Such couples q_r, q_s constitute the conditions for equivalence for q_i and q_j, since the relation $q_i \equiv q_j$ requires that q_r and q_s be also equivalent.

The table is then updated as follows: if the couple q_r, q_s appears in cell (q_i, q_j), and a cross appears in cell (q_r, q_s), a cross is also entered in (q_i, q_j). This process is orderly iterated on all the cells of the table, until no further updating is possible. Then, every cell non containing a cross indicates the equivalence between the corresponding states. From such information the equivalence classes are easily constructed, by grouping all the states pairwise equivalent.

The formal justification of the Paull and Unger procedure (that is, the proof that the final configuration of the table gives the correct equivalences) is based on an inverse of proposition 1 for a single automaton. Namely:

Proposition 2. Let q_i and q_j be states of automaton A. Then, $q_i \equiv q_j$ if and only if

$$\delta(q_i, x_h) = \delta(q_j, x_h)$$
$$\lambda(q_i, x_h) \equiv \lambda(q_j, x_h)$$

for every input x_h.

By theorem 1, the procedure converges in a number of passes $\leq n-1$.

Exercise. Find a reasonable pictorial form for displaying the equivalence table.

Exercise. Using the table of previous exercise, apply the Paull and Unger procedure to finding a minimal form automaton equivalent to the following:

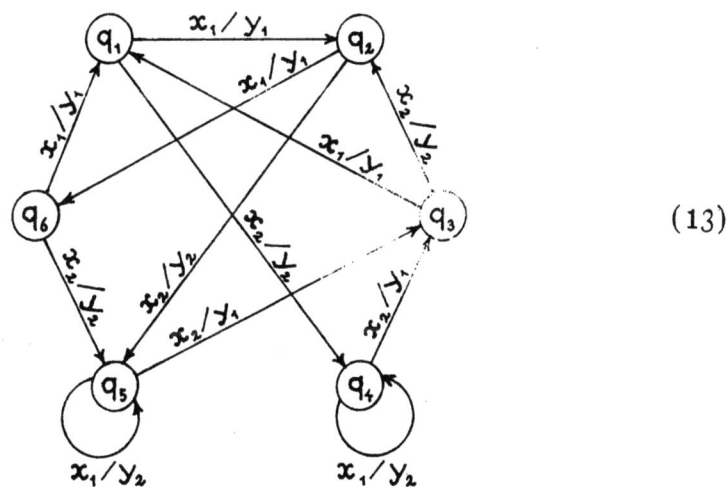

(13)

We conclude this section with some remarks on the notion of automaton equivalence. If seen at the light of system theory, definition 5 is particularly restrictive. In fact, it depends upon definition 4, which rules state equivalence through the identity of output reactions of two states to any input sequence.

A less restrictive definition can be posed, if the state s of S to be equivalent to state p of P is chosen as a function of the particular input sequence x_h^*. That is, given p and x_h^*, the outputs generated from p and s are identical, while such a property may not hold for $x_k^* = x_h^*$.

More specifically:

Definition 7. Two automata P and S are <u>weakly equivalent</u> if, for any state $p \in Q_P$ and any input sequence x^*, there is a state $s \in Q_S$ such that:

$$\delta_P(p, x^*) = \delta_S(s, x^*) ,$$

and vice versa.

An example of weak equivalence is exhibited by the two automata:

(14)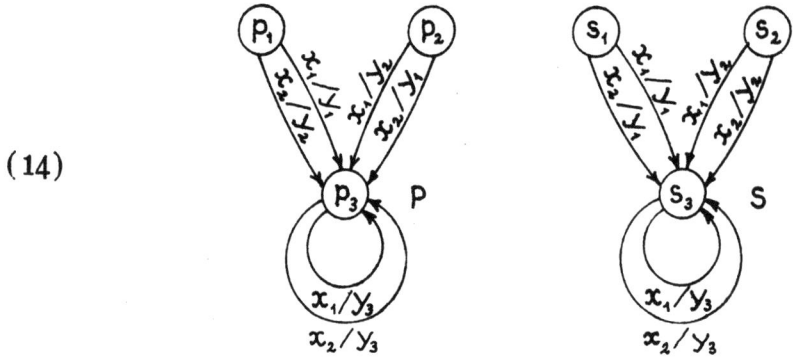

where the correspondences of states are as follows:

s_1 corresponds to p_1, for any x^* beginning with x_1;
s_2 " " p_1 " " " " " x_2
s_2 " " p_2 " " " " " x_1
s_1 " " p_2 " " " " " x_2,
s_3 " " p_3 " " ";

and the same correspondences hold between states p_i and s_j, for the "vice versa" of definition 7.

However, P and S of (14) are not equivalent, since no state of S is equivalent to p_1 or to p_2 (and no state of P is equivalent to s_1 or s_2).

The relationship between equivalence and weak equivalence of automata is demonstrated in the following proposition:

Proposition 3. If automata P and S are weakly equivalent and strongly connected, then they are equivalent.

Proposition 3, although not formulated in such a simple form, is implicitly present in Ginsburg [3] (theorem 1.4 and following topics).

Exercise. Find a good sense justification of proposition 3. (A thorough examination of example (14) may be a good start.)

4. Controllability and observability

The notions of controllability and observability play a primary role in System Theory. In this section, we shall develope them briefly for the special case of automata. In this respect, an ordered presentation of some results about automaton experimentation will be of great help.

Controllability takes a simple form in connection with automata, merely being related to the possibility of finding an input sequence capable of bringing the automaton from the present state, to a particular designated state $\bar{q}$. If compared to the parallel notion in the calssical theory of controllability, $\bar{q}$ has the meaning of "zero state".

Definition 8. Automaton A is <u>controllable in state q_i</u>, if and only if there exists an input sequence x^* such that

$$\lambda(q_i, x^*) = \bar{q} .$$

Automaton A is <u>controllable</u> if and only if it is controllable in every state.

For example, automaton (5) is controllable if q_1 is selected as $\bar{q}$. It is not controllable if q_4 is selected as $\bar{q}$.

The relationship between controllability and connectedness is expressed by the assertion:

Assertion 2. (Arbib [5], Ch. 6). If every state of automaton A is reachable from $\bar{q}$, then being A controllable implies that A is strongly connected.

In order to state the <u>optimal control problem</u> for automata (Arbib [5], Ch. 6), a suitable <u>cost function</u> must be defined. For a given automaton $A = (X, Y, Q, \lambda, \delta)$ and a set of costs C, a cost function c for A has the form:

$$c : Q \times X \longrightarrow C$$

where $c(q_i, x_h)$ gives the cost of transition from state q_i to state $\lambda(q_i, x_h)$. The definition of c can be extended as:

$$c : Q \times X^* \longrightarrow C$$

by postulating the additivity of costs:

$$c(q_i, x_h^* x_k^*) = c(q_i, x_h^*) + c(\lambda(q_i, x_h^*), x_k^*) .$$

Then, the optimal control problem can be posed as:

Problem. Given automaton A in state q_i, find an input sequence x^* such that:

i. $\lambda(q_i, x^*) = \bar{q}$ ($\bar{q}$ is the designated terminal state);

ii. $\lambda(q_i, x_h^*) \neq \bar{q}$ for any x_h^* such that $x_h^* x_k^* = x^*$, with x_k^* non void;

iii. $c(q_i, x^*)$ is minimal.

If interpreted on the graph representation of the automaton, such a problem is classically solved by the optimal path techniques of dynamic programming [2].

More complex is the notion of observability for automata: in fact, much more complex than probably expected by the reader familiar with the theory of linear systems.

A preliminary concept of observability of states, to be more formally defined later, is that the (unknown) current state q_i of an automaton A is observable, if q_i can be determined by observing the output reactions of A to suitable input sequences.

Observing the external behavior as above, actually means to conduct an experimentation on A, which must then be carefully defined. Automata studies on this subject were classically aimed to the solution of a slightly different problem (called the "homing problem" by some authors), namely the one of determining the _terminal state_ into which A is taken by the application of a suitable input sequence, when the initial state q_i

is unknown. However, the following results on <u>initial state</u> determination can be extracted from all such studies.

<u>Definition 9.</u> An <u>experiment</u> on automaton A is a collection of pairs x_i^*, y_i^*, $1 \leq i \leq m$ such that:

i. x_i^* is an input sequence;

ii. y_i^* is the output sequence generated by the application of x_i^*;

iii. A starts in the same state for all the x_i^*, although such a state is unknown.

The length of the longest sequence x_i^* is the <u>length</u> of the experiment.

m is the size of the experiment.

An experiment of size 1 is a <u>simple</u> experiment.

Related to previous definitions of equivalence (Defs. 5 and 7), the notion of experiment has a particular relevance. In fact, we can state that:

1. Two automata P and S are equivalent, if they are indistinguishable by any experiment.

   That is, for any experiment on P starting in the unknown state p, there is a state s of S yielding the same experiment, and vice versa.

2. Two automata P and S are weakly equivalent, if they are indistinguishable by any simple experiment.

We can now put the following definition, giving a precise relation between observability and experiments.

Observability and experimentation   31
_____

Definition 10. Automaton A is <u>observable in state</u> q_i, if q_i can
    be determined by some experiment on A starting in q_i. Auto-
    maton A is <u>observable</u> if and only if it is observable in eve-
    ry state.

            In the light of this definition, a classical re-
sult of System Theory can be extended to automata. Namely:
Proposition 4. Necessary and sufficient condition for automaton
    A to be observable, is that A is in minimal form.

            The validity of Proposition 4 relies upon the very
general definition of observability (Definition 10), where no
constraint was put on the experiment to be used for determining
q_i. Bounds on the length and size of such experiment have been
implicitly derived by Ginsburg [3]. Some of his results are
summarized in the following proposition:
Proposition 5. An automaton A in minimal form is observable in
    any state q_i, by performing an experiment of length $\leq n - 1$
    and of size $\leq n - 1$, where n is the number of states of A.

            Then, for less powerful experiments than the one
of Proposition 5, the automaton may not be observable even if it
is in minimal form. For example, the following automaton (Arbib
[5], Ch. 6):

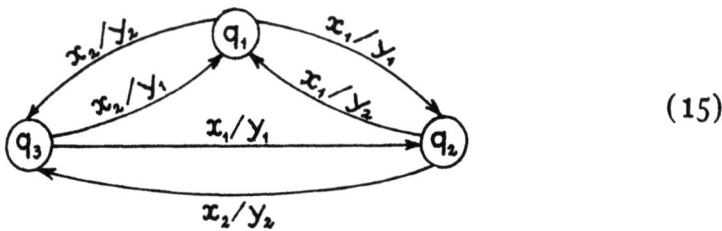   (15)

is in minimal form, but is not observable by simple experiments. In fact, no input sequence beginning with x_1 can discriminate between q_1 and q_2; no input sequence beginning with x_2 can discriminate between q_1 and q_2; hence, no input sequence can insure whether the automaton was in q_1 or not.

In fact, automaton (15) is observable by performing experiments of size 2 (Proposition 5). The reader may verify this point by himself.

5. Incomplete automata.

The automaton studied thus far, as it appears in definition 1, is complete; that is, the next state and output are specified for each possible state and input.

However, this condition turns out not to be the most general, nor the most common in practical cases. In fact, whenever the automaton is used in synthesis problems, as to model the behavior of a system to be designed, there may well be some pairs of state and input q_i, x_h for which either $\lambda(q_i, x_h)$ or $\delta(q_i, x_h)$ is not defined. Such an automaton is called incomplete. Its formal definition is as follows:

Definition 11. An incomplete automaton A is a quintuple:

(16)
$$A = (X, Y, Q, \lambda, \delta)$$

where:

X is the finite set of inputs;

Y is the finite set of autputs;

Q is the finite set of states;

λ is a mapping of a subset Λ of $Q \times X$ into Q;

that is

$$\lambda : \Lambda \to Q, \quad \Lambda \subseteq Q \times X ;$$

δ is a mapping of a subset Δ of $Q \times X$ onto Q;

that is:

Obviously, the (complete) automaton of definition 1 is a particular case of the more general incomplete automaton.

As it will be seen, several concepts about automata become vastly more complex if the hypothesis of completeness is removed. For a correct understanding of the new problems arising for an automaton A, the reasons for the incompleteness of A must be clearly examined. They may be of either of the three following types:

1. Application of input x_h to A in state q_i is <u>forbidden</u>.
Then

$$q_i, x_h \notin \Lambda , \quad q_i, x_h \notin \Delta$$

that is, both next state and output are left unspecified.

2. Input x_h should never appear when A is in state q_i : if x_h does appear, this corresponds to an <u>error</u> in the input sequence. Then

$$q_i, x_h \notin \Lambda , \quad q_i, x_h \notin \Delta .$$

However, if the detection of such an error is required, a new output $\bar{\bar{y}}$ may be inserted in y and regarded as an alarm, and the definition of δ extended as to include: $\delta(q_i, x_h) = \bar{\bar{y}}$. Or a new state $\bar{\bar{q}}$ may be inserted in Q, and λ extended to: $\lambda(q_i, x_h) = \bar{\bar{q}}$.

Note that a unique output $\bar{\bar{y}}$, or a unique state $\bar{\bar{q}}$, may be emplied for all the non specifications of A due to error.

3. If input x_h is applied to A in state q_i, it <u>does not matter</u> which one the next state or the output will be. Then, either one, or both, of the following relations are realized:

$$q_i, x_h \notin \Lambda \quad , \quad q_i, x_h \notin \Delta .$$

In the pictorial representation of the automaton, no arc leaving node q_i and labeled by x_h will be present in the graph, whenever both $\lambda(q_i, x_h)$ and $\delta(q_i, x_h)$ are not defined. If only $\delta(q_i, x_h)$ is not defined, the arc is labeled "$x_h/$". If only $\lambda(q_i, x_h)$ is not defined, an arc pointing nowhere is used.

Let us now derive an example from one of the most proper fields of application: namely, the automaton be regarded as a language translator from input sentences x^* into output sentences y^*. Let the input language be composed of the sentence:

I am great;

and all the ones obtained by the substitutions:

(17)   I am (you are) great (honest - generous);

The input set X is:

An example from the theory of languages

$X = \{$ I, am, you, are, great, honest, generous,;$\}$

but only some input sequences of length four are allowed.

Let the automaton be an English-Italian translator. Then, the corresponding output set Y will be:

$Y = \{$ io, sono, tu, sei, grande, onesto, generoso,;$\}$

and the automaton will have the form:

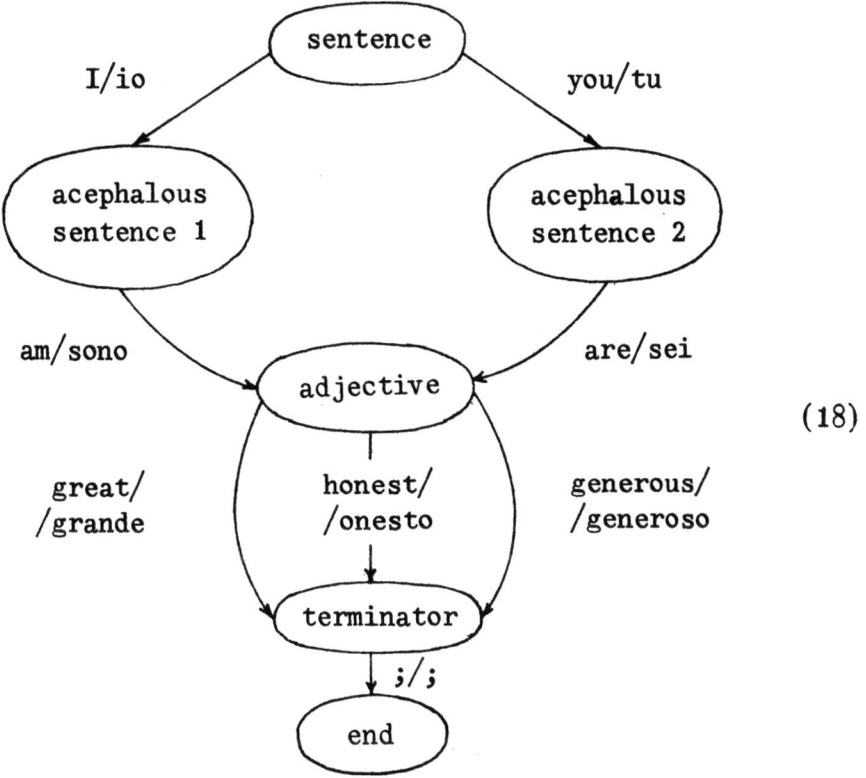

(18)

The automaton must be started in the initial state "sentence", and terminates in state "end" whenever the input sentence is correct. The Italian translation is generated at the output.

5. Incomplete automata

Clearly, (18) is an incomplete automaton, since it does not include arcs corresponding to incorrect input appearances in the sentence to be translated. That is, we are in presence of non specifications of above type 2, where both λ and δ are not defined for given state - input pairs. As already suggested, a new output $\bar{\bar{y}}$ = ERROR may be included in Y to indicate incorrect inputs, and the automaton modified as follows: (*)

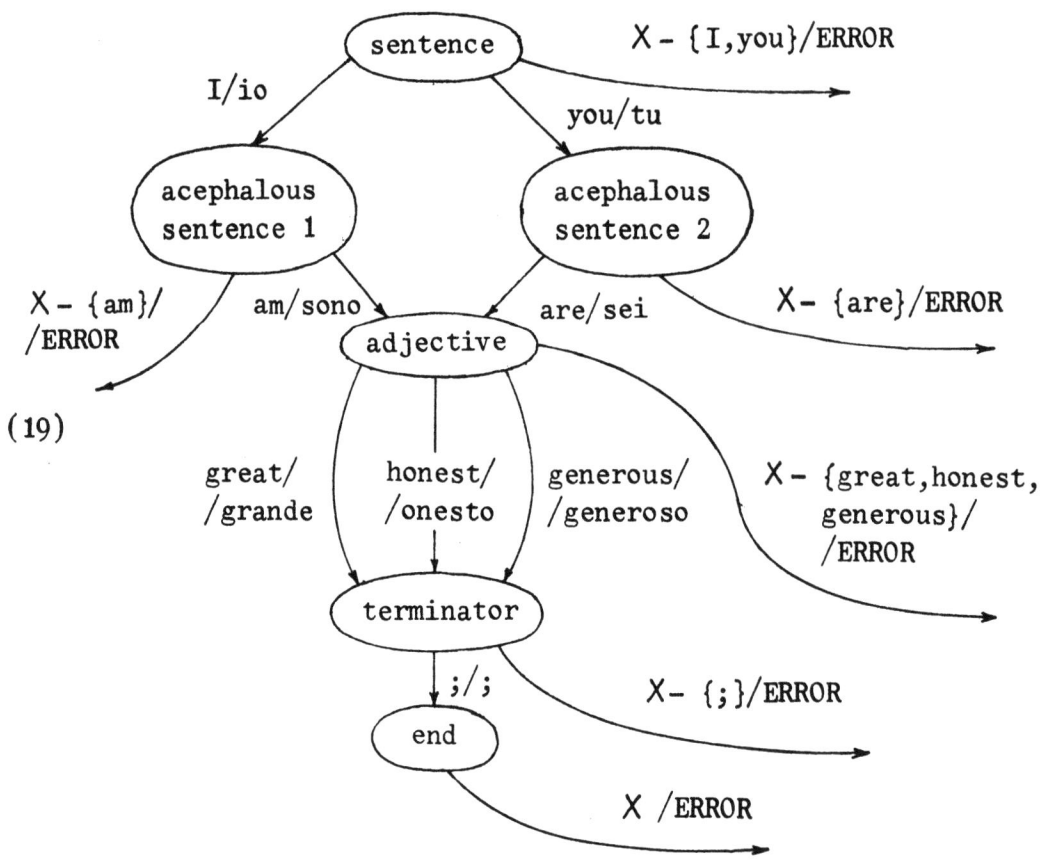

(19)

(*) For semplicity, a single arc per node has been added to the./.

(19) is still incomplete, since the next state is not defined whenever an incorrect input occurs.

A first difficulty is encoutered in the study of incomplete automata, when an extension of the definition of λ and δ from inputs to input sequences is tried. Since some intermediate states may be unspecified, a straightforward extension such as the one used for complete automata (relations (3)) is unusable. In fact, a new concept is to be defined:

Definition 12. An input sequence $x^* = x_1, x_2, \ldots, x_k$ is appli-
cable to automaton A in state q, if each state $q_1 = q$, $q_{i+1} = \lambda(q_i, x_i)$ for $1 \leq i \leq k-1$ is defined in A. (**)

The output sequence y^* generated by A in response to x^* may have some unspecified elements. Such elements are usually indicated by dashes (then, the symbol "-" should be inserted in Y), and must be considered as existing in any respect.

6. Inclusion.

As already illustrated, the notion of equivalence is the key for comparison of the external behavior of complete automata, and ultimately for the minimization of a given complete automaton. However, if incompleteness is considered, it is not

---

graph, indicating all the incorrect input alternatives from such a node.

(**) The definition of applicable input sequence used here differs from the classical one. (See Ginsburg [3]. Ch. 2.1).

6. Inclusion

significant that two output sequences be equal in coincidence with unspecified elements. Then, the notion of equivalence must be replaced by most general and intrigued concepts.

Let P and S be incomplete automata (possibly, P coincident with S), such that $X_P = X_S$.

Definition 13. A state p of P is <u>included</u> by a state s of S if every input sequence x^* applicable to P in p is also applicable to S in s, and the corresponding output sequences y_P^* and y_s^* are identical wherever y_P^* is specified.

In symbols, the inclusion is indicated as $p \leqslant s$. The intuitive meaning of the relation is that, for any given x^*, y_s^* carries the whole information that y_P^* does, and is in general more densely specified than y_P^*.

In the following automaton:

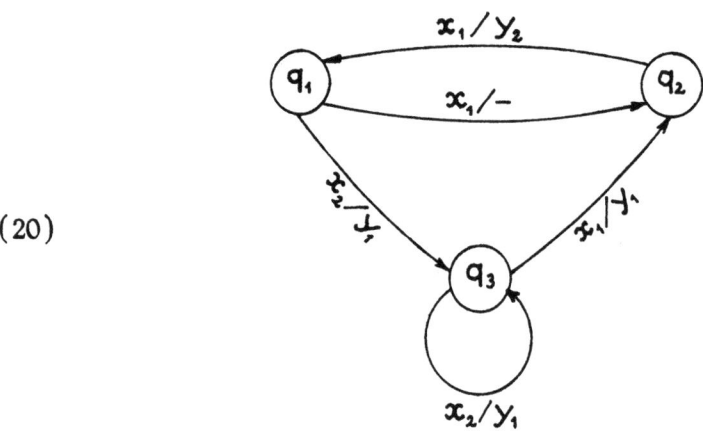

(20)

the relation holds:

$$q_1 \leqslant q_3 ,$$

since any (applicable) input sequence beginning with x_2 yields the same output sequence for both states; any sequence beginning with x_1 yields equal output sequences, except for the first element which is "−" for q_1, and "y_1" for q_3. Instead, no inclusion can be defined between q_1 and q_2, since all the input sequences applicable to q_2 are also applicable to q_1, but the output sequences are more densely specified for the former state.

The relation of inclusion can be extended to automata.

Definition 14. Automaton P is <u>included</u> by automaton S if and only if for each state p of P there is a state s of S, such that $p \leqslant s$.

In symbols, the inclusion between automata is still indicated as $P \leqslant S$. Its intuitive meaning is that S performs any task that P does.

Such a relation is of crucial importance for the minimization problem. In fact, for an incomplete automaton A the above problem can be formulated as the one of finding an automaton A' with minimal number of states, such that $A \leqslant A'$. As it will be seen, there may be more than one such automaton.

Minimization of A is still centered on a merging process for its states. However, a new relation specified in the following definition substitutes the equivalence, for the determination of states that can be merged into a single one.

Definition 15. States q_i and q_j of automaton A are <u>compatible</u>

if, for every input sequence x^* applicable to A in q_i and in q_j, the corresponding output sequences y_i^* and y_j^* are identical, wherever both are specified.

In symbols, compatibility is indicated as $q_i \cong q_j$. Between states of a single automaton, compatibility is a less restrictive relation than inclusion. That is, for every pair of states such that $q_i \leq q_j$, it is also $q_i \cong q_j$.

For example, in automaton (20) both relations hold:

$$q_1 \cong q_3 \;, \qquad q_1 \cong q_2 \;.$$

From definition 15, it clearly follows that the properties are valid:

$q_i \cong q_i$ for every state q_i (reflexivity);

if $q_i \cong q_j$ then $q_j \cong q_i$ (symmetry).

However, the transitive property does not hold for compatibility. For example, in automaton (20) q_2 and q_3 are not compatible.

Then, $\cong$ is not an algebraic equivalence relation. We may still define the <u>compatibility classes</u> of states, as the (largest) classes whose members are all pairwise compatible. However, such classes do not consitute a partition of the set of states Q, since the intersection of any two such classes need not be void. For automaton (20), the compatibility classes are:

$$\{q_1, q_3\} \;; \quad \{q_1, q_2\} \;;$$

whose intersection is $\{q_1\}$.

Exercise. Construct an incomplete automaton for which the number of compatibility classes is larger than the number of states.

Exercise. Derive a lower bound for the number of states of an automaton having the property specified in the previous exercise.

The following proposition, showing an important property of compatibility, is an extension of proposition 1 to a single incomplete automaton.

Proposition 6. Let q_i and q_j be states of automaton A, $q_i \cong q_j$. Then, for any applicable input sequence x^*, the states into which A is led by the application of x^* starting in q_i and q_j are also compatible, if both specified.

Classes of states whose members are all pairwise compatible (i.e., compatibility classes and their subclasses) will be called c-classes. In particular, any class containing exactly one state is a c-class. c-classes are relevant to the minimization problem, which will be solved through the selection of a proper collection of such classes. In order to discuss this point, some terminology is needed.

For a given automaton A, a collection of c-classes is complete if every state of A is contained in at least one class of the collection.

Given a c-class

$$C = \{q_1, q_2, \ldots, q_s\}$$

let C_i be the class of all the distinct specified states among

$$\lambda(q_1, x_i), \lambda(q_2, x_i), \ldots, \lambda(q_s, x_i);$$

we say that C_i is <u>implied</u> by C. By proposition 6, any implied class C_i is a c-class (i.e., all the states in C_i must be pairwise compatible). In the example (20), the classes implied by $C = \{q_1, q_3\}$ are:

$$C_1 = \{q_2\} \quad ; \quad C_2 = \{q_3\}.$$

A collection of c-classes is <u>closed</u> if, for any class C of the collection, every implied class C_i is contained in at least one class of the collection.

A <u>minimal collection</u> of c-classes is a complete and closed collection with minimum number of classes.

<u>Assertion 3.</u> For any incomplete automaton A, an automaton A' with minimum number of states, such that $A \leq A'$, can be constructed by associating the states of A' to the members of a minimal collection of c-classes of A.

Inputs and outputs of A' are consequently assigned.

For automaton (20), a minimal collection of c-classes is:

$$\{q_1, q_3\} \quad , \quad \{q_2\}$$

and a minimum state automaton that includes (20) correspondently

Determining the C-classes

is:

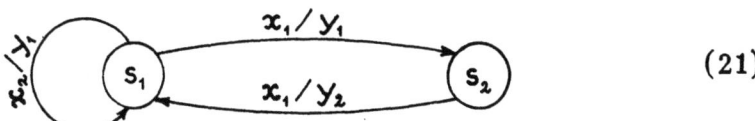
(21)

whose states s_1 and s_2 are respectively derived from $\{q_1, q_3\}$ and $\{q_2\}$. (21) is still incomplete, although more densely specified than (20).

However, also

$$\{q_1, q_3\} \quad , \quad \{q_1, q_2\}$$

is a minimal collection for (20), and a second minimum state automaton that includes (20) can be derived.

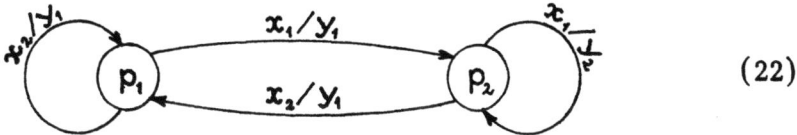
(22)

by associating its states p_1 and p_2 to $\{q_1, q_3\}$ and $\{q_1, q_2\}$ respectively. Note that (22) is a complete automaton.

<u>Exercise.</u> (important) Compare the terminal behavior of automata (20), (21) and (22), by studying the output sequences generated in response to input sequences of your choice.

A crucial point in the minimization problem is the derivation of all the c-classes, from among which a minimal collection is to be extracted. Then, all the compatibility relations between couples of states must be first determined.

For such a purpose, note that the following exten

sion of proposition 2 can be derived from the definition of compatibility.

Proposition 7. Let q_i and q_j be states of automaton A. Then $q_i \cong q_j$ if and only if

$$\delta(q_i, x_h) = \delta(q_j, x_h)$$

for every input x_h for which both next states are specified; and

$$\lambda(q_i, x_h) \cong \lambda(q_j, x_h)$$

for every input x_h for which both next states are specified.

Based on proposition 7, the Paull and Unger procedure illustrated in section 3 applies almost unchanged to the determination of compatibilities. (*) The table will be called compatibility table, since $\cong$ substitutes $\equiv$ in its interpretation. In determining the initial compatibilities on the table, matching of two outputs is considered to be met if one or both outputs are unspecified. Updating of the table is identical to the complete case.

In the present case also, the procedure converges in a number of passes $\leq n-1$, where n is the number of states of the automaton. At the end of the process, the table gives all the compatibilities between states. All the c-classes are

---

(*) Actually, the procedure was developped by its authors for the specific case of incomplete machines.

Extension of the previous linguistic application   45

easily derived from such information.

Exercise. Find a minimum state automaton that includes the following one:

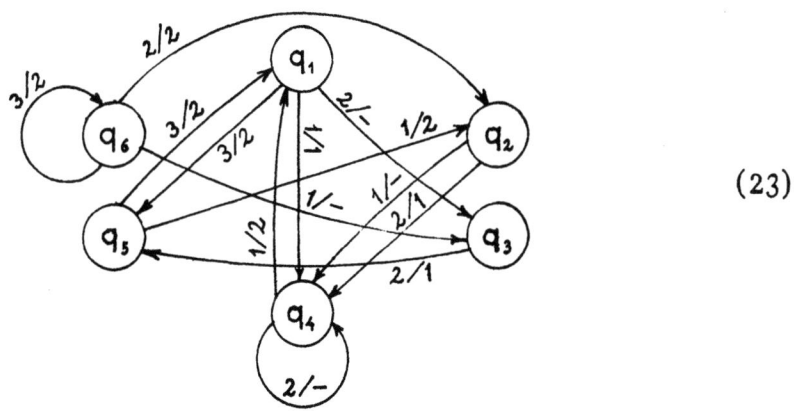
(23)

Application. Let us extend the language (17), as to allow the appearence of two adjectives linked by the conjunction "and". That is, all the sentences:

I am (you are) great (honest –generous);   (17)

I am (you are) great (honest – generous) and great (honest– generous);   (24)

will be now correct. The English-Italian translator takes the new form:

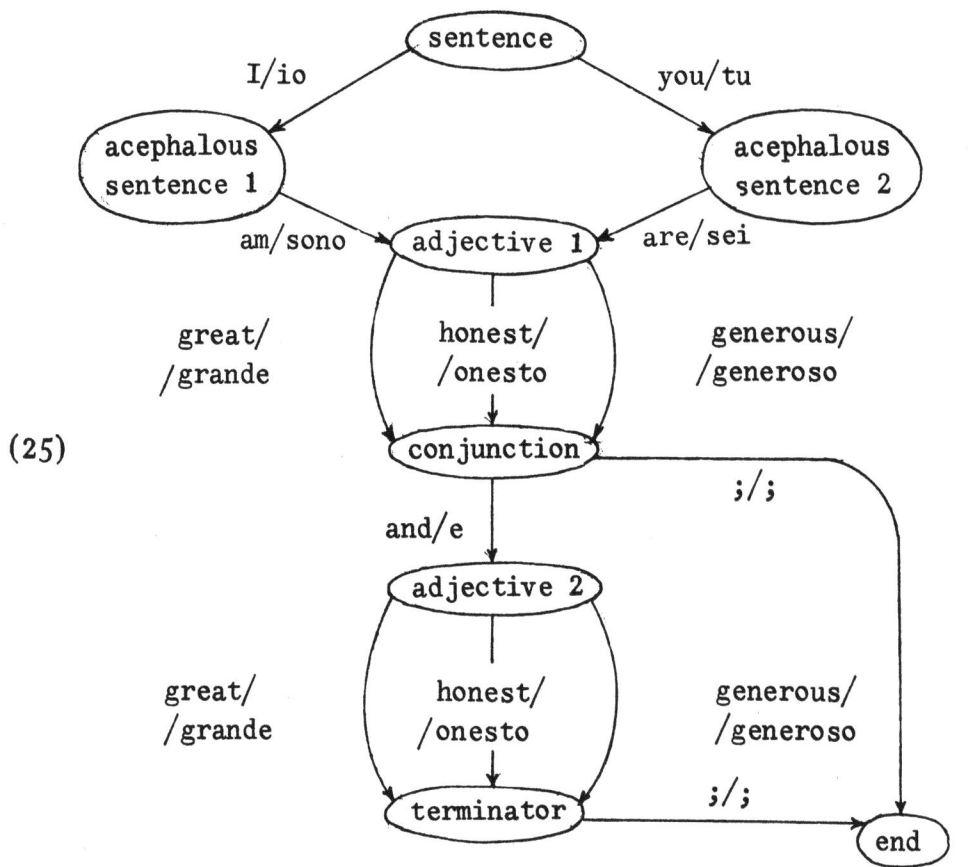

(25)

All the non specifications of (25) correspond to incorrect appearences of elements in the input sentence. If (25) is completed by specifying the new outputs $\bar{\bar{y}}$ = ERROR (as already done in (19)), no two states of the automaton are compatible. Hence, no state reduction for the translator is possible.

Let us now further extend the input language, as to include concatenations of adjectives of any length.

Automaton (25) can be modified to process the new language, by including a transition between states "terminator" and "adjective 2", for input "and". That is, the corresponding

Continuation of the application

section of (25) is transformed as:

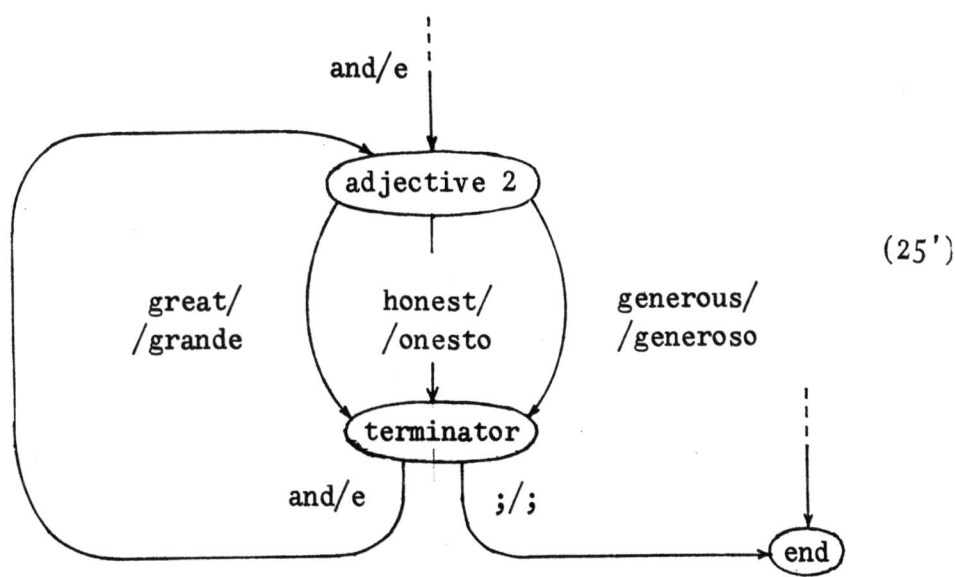

(25')

In automaton (25)-(25') states "conjunction" and "terminator" are clearly compatible. Consequently, "adjective 1" and "adjective 2" are also compatible (proposition 7), and the compatibility classes of states are:

{sentence}, {acephalous sentence 1}, {acephalous sentence 2}, {adjective 1, adjective 2}, {conjunction, terminator}, {end}.

Then, the following minimum state translator can be constructed (with obvious associations between -classes of (25)-(25') and states of (26):

(26)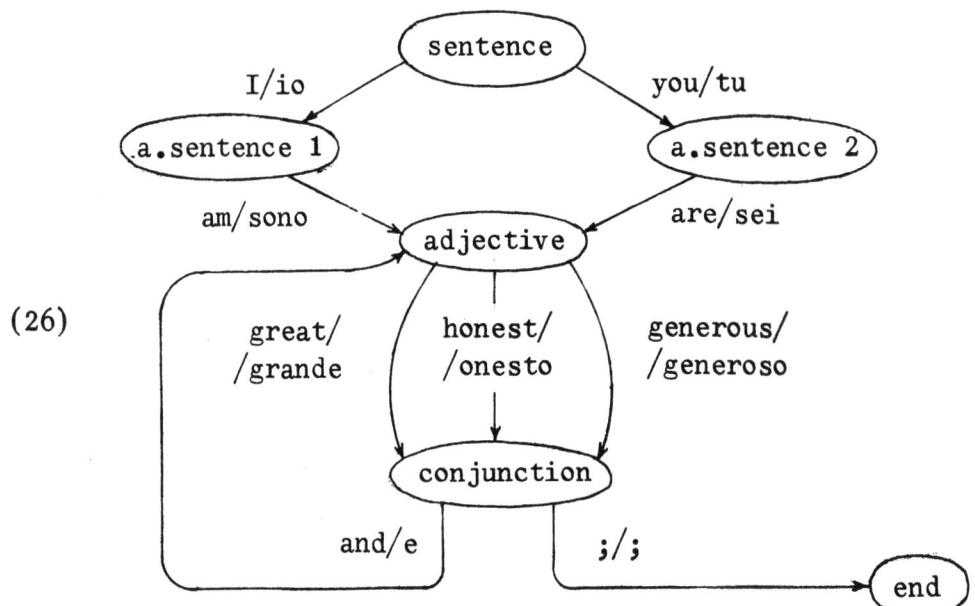

Note that (26) is a finite automaton, which is able to accept input sequences of non finite length.

Exercise (difficult). Find a justification to the fact that automaton (25) is more complex than automaton (26), while it accepts a subset of the input sequences of the latter.

Although the Paull and Unger procedure is a systematic tool for the determination of all c-classes, the selection of a minimal collection from among them remains a cumbersome problem, if a completely enumerative approach is used. Advantage in this respect can be taken from a reduction of the number of c--classes to be considered, that can be achieved along the following lines.

Given a c-class C, the class set P_C implied by C is the set of all classes C_i implied by C such that:

i. C_i has at least two elements:
ii. $C_i \not\subset C$;
iii. $C_i \not\subset C_j$ if $C_j \in P_c$.

P_c expresses all the significant conditions for closure imposed by C, if C is a member of the collection.

A c-class D is <u>excluded</u> by another c-class C, if:
i. $C \supset D$;
ii. $P_c \subseteq P_D$.

<u>Definition 16.</u> A <u>prime c-class</u> is one that is not excluded by any other c-class.

The following theorem restricts to prime c-classes the set of c-classes to be considered for the selection of a minimal collection.

<u>Theorem 2</u> (Grasselli and Luccio [4]). The members of at least one minimal collection are prime c-classes.

For example, consider the following portion of automaton:

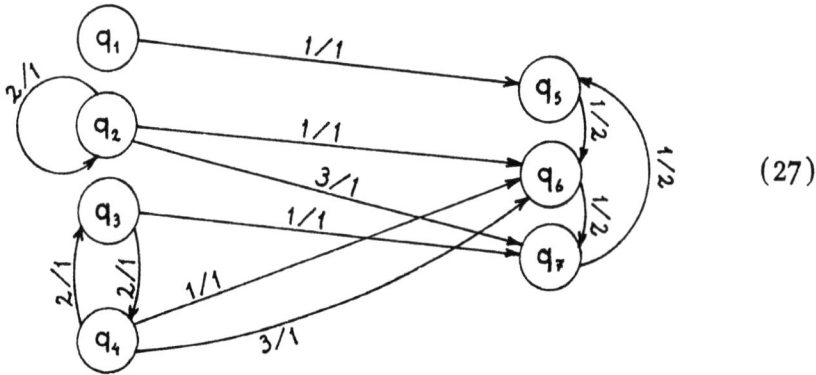

(27)

$C = \{q_1, q_2, q_3, q_4\}$ is a compatibility class, that implies c-classes $C_1 = \{q_5, q_6, q_7\}$, $C_2 = \{q_2, q_3, q_4\}$ and $C_3 = \{q_6, q_7\}$. Since $C_2 \subset C$ and $C_3 \subset C_1$, only C_1 is a member of the class set P_C implied by C.

Similarly, class sets for the subclasses of C can be determined. Two such class sets are listed below:

              c-class   implied class set

$$C = \{q_1, q_2, q_3, q_4\} \quad \{q_5, q_6, q_7\}$$

(28) $\quad D = \{q_1, q_2, q_3\} \quad \{q_5, q_6, q_7\}$

$$E = \{q_1, q_2, q_4\} \quad \{q_5, q_6\}, \{q_2, q_3\}, \{q_6, q_7\}$$

Clearly, D is excluded by C and need not be considered for the minimality problem. Instead, E is not excluded by C.

Note that compatibility class $F = \{q_5, q_6, q_7\}$ implies itself only, hence its class set is void:

              c-class   implied class set

(28') $\quad F = \{q_5, q_6, q_7\} \quad \emptyset$

Then, every subclass of F is excluded by F and need not be considered.

The number of c-classes to be retained for selecting a minimal collection can be further reduced over the one of prime c-classes, if a technique for class set updating is used.

In the above example, once the subclass $\{q_5, q_6\}$ has been excluded by F, the class set of E can be consequently updated. In fact, the closure requirement that q_5 and q_6 be contained in the same class of the minimal collection, is now met by imposing the presence in such a collection of class $\{q_5, q_6, q_7\}$, which is the only prime c-class containing the above two states. Then, the class set of E is changed to:

$$\begin{array}{ccc} \text{c-class} & & \text{implied class set} \\ E = \{q_1, q_2, q_4\} & \{q_5, q_6, q_7\}, & \{q_2, q_3\} \end{array} \quad (29)$$

(class $\{q_6, q_7\}$ appearing in (28) has been cancelled from the class set, since is included in $\{q_5, q_6, q_7\}$).

As a consequence, c-class E is now excluded by C and can be eliminated.

A process of such kind is obviously iterative. Details on its application, leading to a general extended definition of prime classes can be found in Luccio [7].

7. Extensions

We conclude these notes by indicating some possible extensions of the notions discussed thus far, on which more work is to be done.

In the definition of incomplete automata (section 5), the notion of unspecified next state was introduced: the transition to an unspecified state may be interpreted as the transition to any state.

This concept may be further extended if, for any input-state pair, a subset of possible next states is specified. That is, λ becomes a mapping from $Q \times X$ onto a set of subsets of Q. An automaton with such a structure is called non deterministic. Clearly, complete and incomplete automata are particular cases of non deterministic automata.

Note that no concept of probability is associated to the different possible transitions defined for any input-state pair, but all such transitions are considered to take place. In the graph representation of the automaton, different operating points move along the branches contemporarily. Then, different output sequences would correspond to a single input sequence.

However, non deterministic automata have not been studied in general as input/output translators, but merely as recognition devices [3]. That is, their role is simply to recognize wether an input sequence is correct in a given input language. For such a purpose, no output set is defined, but an initial and a final state are designated: the input sequence, if correct, must lead the operating point from one to the other.

For example, the following is a non deterministic automaton for the recognition of all words containing a double consonant (e.g., BB, CC etc.): the input set is coincident with the English alphabet:

Applications and extensions   53

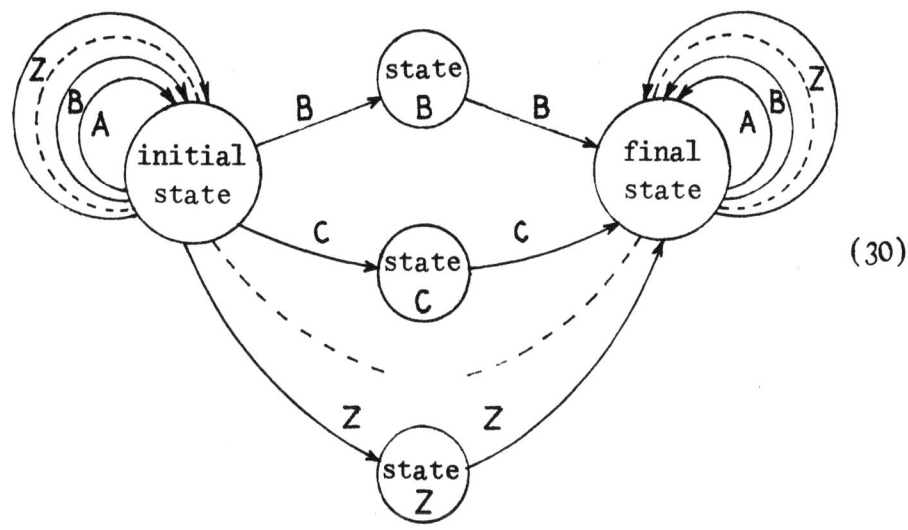

(30)

Note that more than one branch labeled with the same input leaves from any node (e.g., branch labeled "B" from the "initial state"). Note further that all the non specified next states correspond to errors (e.g., next state of "state B" for input "A"), thus blocking the possible movement of one operating point.

<u>Exercise</u>. Check the functioning of (30), by trying on it a correct and an incorrect input sequence (e.g., MAMMA and PRETE).

<u>Exercise</u> (voluntary). Find a deterministic automaton that performs the task of (30).

   Developing theories of non deterministic automata seen as input/output translators is still an open field of study.(*)

(*) A general study for the minimization of automata of such a type will be published in the near future. (R.E. Miller - Personal communication).

A second field worth to be investigated is the one of controllability and observability for incomplete and non deterministic automata.

Finally, a very interesting extension is to remove the assumption for the automaton to be stationary (section 2), to study the theory of automata wtih variable structure.

REFERENCES

[1] M.A. Arbib. Theories of abstract automata. Prentice Hall, Englewood Cliffs, 1969.

[2] R. Bellman and S. Dreyfus. Applied dynamic Programming. Princeton University Press, Princeton, 1962

[3] S. Ginsburg. An introduction to mathematical machine theory. Addison Wesley, Reading, 1962.

[4] A. Grasselli and F. Luccio. A method for minimizing the number of internal states in incompletely specified sequential networks, IEEE Transactions on Electronic Computers, Vol. EC-14, June 1965, 350--359.

[5] R.E. Kalman, P.L. Falb and M.A. Arbib. Topics in mathematical system theory. Part 3. McGrow Hill, New York, 1969.

[6] F. Luccio. Reduction of the number of columns in flow table minimization. IEEE Transaction on Electronic Computers, Vol. EC-15, October 1966, 803-805.

[7] F. Luccio. Extending the definition of prime compatibility classes of states in incomplete sequential machine reduction. IEEE Transactions on Computers, Vol. C-18, June 1969, 537-540.

ADDITIONAL BIBLIOGRAPHY

M.A. Arbib. Brains, machines and mathematics. McGraw Hill, New York, 1964.
    See this book for the role of automata theory in neurophisiology and cybernetics.

J.E. Hopcroft and J.D. Ullman. Formal languages and their relation to automata. Addison Wesley, Reading, 1969.
    See this book for the linguistic interpretation and application of automata.

CONTENTS

	Page
Preface	3
1. Introduction: Automata and Systems	5
2. The notion of state	6
3. Equivalence and minimization	14
4. Controllability and observability	27
5. Incomplete automata	32
6. Inclusion	37
7. Extensions	51
References	55

If you have any concerns about our products,
you can contact us on
ProductSafety@springernature.com

In case Publisher is established outside the EU,
the EU authorized representative is:
**Springer Nature Customer Service Center GmbH
Europaplatz 3, 69115 Heidelberg, Germany**

Printed by Libri Plureos GmbH
in Hamburg, Germany